Kids Daily Plan

This Planner Belongs to

____

____

Daily Plan

Date
__ / __ / __

Top 3 Priorities

Importan Times

Other to-do's

Food and Drink

Exercise

Notes

Daily Plan

Top 3 Priorities

Importan Times

Other to-do's

Food and Drink

Exercise

Notes

Daily Plan

Date __ / __ / ____

Top 3 Priorities

Importan Times

Other to-do's

Food and Drink

Exercise

Notes

Daily Plan

Top 3 Priorities

Importan Times

Other to-do's

Food and Drink

Exercise

Notes

Daily Plan

Date
-- / -- / ----

Top 3 Priorities

Importan Times

Other to-do's

Food and Drink

Exercise

Notes

Daily Plan

Date
__ / __ / ____

Top 3 Priorities

★ --------------------------------
★ --------------------------------
★ --------------------------------

Importan Times

★ --------------------------------
★ --------------------------------
★ --------------------------------

Other to-do's

Food and Drink

Exercise

Notes

Daily Plan

Top 3 Priorities

Importan Times

Other to-do's

Food and Drink

Exercise

Notes

Daily Plan

Date

__ / __ / ____

Top 3 Priorities

Importan Times

Other to-do's

Food and Drink

Exercise

Notes

Daily Plan

Top 3 Priorities

Importan Times

Other to-do's

Food and Drink

Exercise

Notes

Daily Plan

Date
__ / __ / ____

____

Top 3 Priorities

★ ______________________________

★ ______________________________

★ ______________________________

Importan Times

★ ______________________________

★ ______________________________

★ ______________________________

Other to-do's

____

____

____

____

____

____

____

____

____

____

Food and Drink

____

____

____

____

____

Exercise

____

____

____

Notes

____

____

____

____

Daily Plan

Top 3 Priorities

★ ________________________________
★ ________________________________
★ ________________________________

Importan Times

★ ________________________________
★ ________________________________
★ ________________________________

Other to-do's

____
____
____
____
____
____
____
____
____

Food and Drink

____
____
____
____
____

Exercise

____
____
____

Notes

____
____
____
____

Daily Plan

Date __ / __ / ___

Top 3 Priorities

★ -----------------------
★

★

Importan Times

★
★

★

Other to-do's

Food and Drink

Exercise

Notes

Daily Plan

Date
__ / __ / ____

____

Top 3 Priorities

Importan Times

Other to-do's

Food and Drink

Exercise

Notes

Daily Plan

Date

__ / __ / ____

____

Top 3 Priorities

★ ____________________

★ ____________________

★ ____________________

Importan Times

★ ____________________

★ ____________________

★ ____________________

Other to-do's

____

____

____

____

____

____

____

____

Food and Drink

____

____

____

____

Exercise

____

____

____

Notes

____

____

____

Daily Plan

Date

--/--/----

Top 3 Priorities

★ ----------------------------------

★ ----------------------------------

★ ----------------------------------

Importan Times

★ ----------------------------------

★ ----------------------------------

★ ----------------------------------

Other to-do's

Food and Drink

Exercise

Notes

Daily Plan

Top 3 Priorities

Importan Times

Other to-do's

Food and Drink

Exercise

Notes

Daily Plan

Date
__ / __ / ___
____

Top 3 Priorities

Importan Times

Other to-do's

Food and Drink

Exercise

Notes

Daily Plan

Date
__ /__/____

____

Top 3 Priorities

★
★
★

Importan Times

★
★
★

Other to-do's

Food and Drink

Exercise

Notes

Daily Plan

Date
__/__/___

Top 3 Priorities

Importan Times

Other to-do's

Food and Drink

Exercise

Notes

Daily Plan

Date
__ /__ /____

Top 3 Priorities

Importan Times

Other to-do's

Food and Drink

Exercise

Notes

Daily Plan

Date

__ / __ / ____

Top 3 Priorities

Importan Times

Other to-do's

Food and Drink

Exercise

Notes

Daily Plan

Dat
__ / __ / ___

Top 3 Priorities

Importan Times

Other to-do's

Food and Drink

Exercise

Notes

Daily Plan

Date

__ / __ / ___

____

Top 3 Priorities

★ ----------------------

★ ----------------------

★ ----------------------

Importan Times

★ ----------------------

★ ----------------------

★ ----------------------

Other to-do's

Food and Drink

Exercise

Notes

Daily Plan

Date
__ / __ / ____

Top 3 Priorities

Importan Times

Other to-do's

Food and Drink

Exercise

Notes

Daily Plan

Date
__ / __ / ___
____

Top 3 Priorities

Importan Times

Other to-do's

Food and Drink

Exercise

Notes

Daily Plan

Date

__ / __ / ____

Top 3 Priorities

Importan Times

Other to-do's

Food and Drink

Exercise

Notes

Daily Plan

Date
__ / __ / ____

Top 3 Priorities

★
★
★

Importan Times

★
★
★

Other to-do's

Food and Drink

Exercise

Notes

Daily Plan

Date
__ / __ / __

Top 3 Priorities

Importan Times

Other to-do's

Food and Drink

Exercise

Notes

Daily Plan

Date
-- / -- / ----

Top 3 Priorities

Importan Times

Other to-do's

Food and Drink

Exercise

Notes

Daily Plan

Date

__ / __ / ____

Top 3 Priorities

Importan Times

Other to-do's

Food and Drink

Exercise

Notes

Daily Plan

Date
__ / __ / ____
____

Top 3 Priorities

★ --
★ --
★ --

Importan Times

★ --
★ --
★ --

Other to-do's

Food and Drink

Exercise

Notes

Daily Plan

Date

__ / __ / ____

Top 3 Priorities

Importan Times

Other to-do's

Food and Drink

Exercise

Notes

Daily Plan

Dat

__ / __ / __

____

Top 3 Priorities

- ⭐ ____________________
- ⭐ ____________________
- ⭐ ____________________

Importan Times

- ⭐ ____________________
- ⭐ ____________________
- ⭐ ____________________

Other to-do's

- ____________________
- ____________________
- ____________________
- ____________________
- ____________________
- ____________________
- ____________________
- ____________________
- ____________________
- ____________________

Food and Drink

____
____
____
____
____

Exercise

____
____
____

Notes

____
____
____

Daily Plan

Date
__ /__ /____
____

Top 3 Priorities

Importan Times

Other to-do's

Food and Drink

Exercise

Notes

Daily Plan

Date
-- / -- / ----

Top 3 Priorities

★ ----------------------
★ ----------------------
★ ----------------------

Importan Times

★ ----------------------
★ ----------------------
★ ----------------------

Other to-do's

Food and Drink

Exercise

Notes